Rent to Own

The Essential Renter's Guide to Home Ownership

David Fenton

eBook version formatted by Writing Nights, www.writingnights.org

Table of Contents

Introduction

I'm a Doctor and a Real Estate Investor. When I first decided I wanted to go into medicine people asked a lot of questions, but there was one question that almost everyone asked. My friends, my family, mentors that I had, my girlfriend and every one of the interviewers in the application process. "Why do you want to go into medicine?" The answer was easy. I wanted to help people. I had no money, no influence and no power, so becoming a doctor was the best way I could think of to do that.

During ridiculously long shifts at the hospital during my training, sometimes 24 or even 36 hours long, I would sometimes ask myself the same question, "Why in the heck did I want to go into medicine?" Thankfully I could come back to that same answer and somehow it would allow me to power through and still treat people with care and compassion.

Almost two decades later people are starting to ask questions again. "Why would you invest in Rent-to-Own?" and "Why would you start your own Rent-to-Own company?" Thankfully I can use a very similar answer. I want to invest in

Real Estate and I want to help people. I want to help people realize their dream of home ownership. It is becoming harder and harder to own a home in Canada and the United States. Average wages have been stagnant for decades, housing prices are increasing faster than wages and faster than general inflation. The government and the lending institutions have made it harder and harder to qualify for mortgage financing, especially after the mortgage crisis in 2008. These factors make it much more difficult for new home buyers to get into that all important first home. Once you own a home, a whole world of financial opportunity opens up to you, usually for the rest of your life (we'll talk more about this in Chapter Two). The problem is qualifying for that first home.

A few facts:

Canada ranks 33rd in home ownership at only 68.6 percent.

The U.S. is 39th at 64.5 percent.

Incidentally, Romania is number 1 at over 96 percent.

Of people in the top 25 percent of income, over 77 percent are homeowners and this percentage is increasing. In the bottom 25 percent of income earners, only 19 percent are homeowners and this number is decreasing. The age of owning a first home is increasing and the majority of new homeowners require two incomes to qualify for a home mortgage.

It has been shown that people who own their home are not only wealthier in retirement but also have the opportunity to build generational wealth. Generational wealth is the ability to pass down money and/or assets, such as a home, through inheritance. This can raise whole families out of poverty or financial hardship.

Rent-to-own is a way to get some of those 33-35 percent of North American non-homeowners into a home of their own and generating wealth for themselves and their families.

Now, I'm being asked even more questions. "Why write a book?" Good question. Until recently it never crossed my mind to write a book. I've written scientific papers in university and in my medical training, and even now as a practicing physician. To be honest I never really enjoyed it. Rent-to-own is one of those things most people don't know about, or if they do, they might have heard that it's a scam and are skeptical about it. I find my biggest job with rent-to-own is educating people about what it is and showing them that done properly it absolutely is not a scam, and is perhaps the easiest and most fail safe way to get into the home of their choice NOW, and on a proven path to ownership in a few short years. Because I was answering the same questions every time I discussed rent-to-own I decided to compile the information in one easy to read book that people could read and refer back to whenever an additional question arose.

I feel the public education system is failing people in a major way when it comes to basic financial education. We are taught what the hypotenuse of a triangle is or the year each province or state joined confederation, but don't know why or how to buy a house. We wrote book reports on: "The Tale of Two Cities," "Nineteen Eighty-Four," "Romeo and Juliet" and "War of the Worlds"; but we don't know what a credit bureau report is and how it can affect every aspect of your life from getting a job, getting a home, getting a car and what interest rate you pay if you do qualify for financing.

I wrote short easy to understand chapters on:

What rent-to-own really is.

Why home ownership is usually better than renting.

Who rent-to-own works best for.

How to recognize and avoid a rent-to-own scam.

And more.

In Chapter Four I put a one-page checklist of the steps involved in the rent-to-own process for quick reference. Also included is a glossary of common terms used specifically in the rent-to-own process.

Full disclosure: I'm Canadian. While this book has been written from a Canadian perspective, the concepts are the same whether in Canada, the United States or most other first world countries. I've added in American concepts where I thought they were important.

My hope is that renters will use this book to educate themselves on the rent-to-own process and consider rent-to-own as a viable strategy to home ownership. If you think this book may be useful for someone you know, please don't keep it a secret. Pass it along to a friend or family member, or pass it along via social media.

If you would like to work with us or you would like more information, you can look us up at:

www.BCRTO.com

Facebook: BC Rent to Own Homes

Chapter One:

What is Rent-to-Own?

Let's start with a very common scenario that we can use as an example for the rest of this book.

Trish and Wayne have been married for three years. They have a one-year old daughter and have a second child on the way. They are tired of renting and moving all the time and would like to set down some roots and own their own home.

They found a nice house close to Wayne's work that is also walking distance to the local community center and a good elementary school.

The price of the house is $300,000 and after talking with a realtor, they felt they could afford the mortgage payments. They got an accepted offer on the house subject to financing and inspection (good advice by the realtor).

When they went to their bank, they were shocked to be turned down for a mortgage. It turns out their credit rating wasn't as good as they thought (they had never actually checked it). They also didn't have a big enough down payment for their bank to qualify them. They thought that as first time homebuyers they would only need a five percent down payment, but their bank, as almost all banks, had recently toughened up their qualification criteria and now require ten percent down payment. They also had not budgeted for closing costs.

Trish and Wayne were crushed and embarrassed. They had to phone their realtor and let them know they couldn't buy the house.

With another child on the way they felt it would be many years before they could afford to buy a home and resigned themselves to be renters for many years to come, if not forever.

We will use this example of Trish and Wayne and a $300,000 house throughout the remainder of the book to illustrate several points.

So what is rent-to-own and how could it be used to help out people like Trish and Wayne?

Rent-to-own (sometimes called lease-to-own, lease options or shortened to RTO or R2O) is a creative financing strategy designed to help renters, often good, hardworking, young families, realize their dream of home ownership. It is most suited for people who, for some reason, do not qualify for a mortgage with one of the big banks or credit unions. We will go into more detail of who rent-to-own is good for in Chapter Five.

Before we get into too much detail about rent-to-own, let's talk about the elephant in the room, as they say. Some of you may have heard that rent-to-own is a scam. You may have read this on the internet or were told this by a realtor or mortgage broker that you have worked with.

Let me tell you emphatically that rent-to-own is not a scam. In fact, it is the fastest way that I know of for people who are struggling to realize their dream of home ownership to become proud homeowners, often in a few short years.

If you work with a reputable rent-to-own company, they will ensure that you have the highest possible chance of success at the end of the program.

Can rent-to-own work out badly? Yes it can. This situation is rare and most often occurs when working with an inexperienced rent-to-own company that, in its eagerness to help out a young family, take on someone who in reality, will be unlikely to qualify for a mortgage three or four years in the future. This usually occurs through inexperience and not malice but unfortunately costs the tenant buyers both time and money if they can't qualify for a mortgage at the end of the program. I've never personally seen a situation where a company purposefully took advantage of a person or family that they knew would not qualify. Theoretically, this could happen, but in my experience, it is extremely rare.

We will talk about how to recognize and avoid rent-to-own scams in Chapter Eight.

Now, let's get back to rent-to-own itself. As I said, rent-to-own is the fastest way that I know of for people to turn around their financial situation and become home owners. It really serves three main purposes:

1. It gets you out of the rental cycle and into the house of your choice now.

2. It gives you time to accumulate a larger down payment so you can eventually qualify for bank financing.

3. It gives you time and specific strategies to repair or establish your credit rating, allowing you to qualify for a mortgage.

There are two main types of Rent-to-Own programs and they are very different from each other. Let's talk about those now.

1. House First Rent-to-Own:

This is the more traditional way of doing rent to own. With this strategy, there is already a house and the seller advertises to find a tenant buyer to rent-to-own the house.

There are a few common scenarios:

The first is that you are already renting a house and your landlord asks if you would like to buy the house or rent-to-own the house. If you absolutely love the house you are renting, this can be a viable option.

The second common scenario with House First Rent-to-Own is when a real estate investor buys a house, fixes it up and tries to either sell the house or rent-to-own the house.

There are several potential problems with the House First Rent-to-Own scenario.

First, your landlord or the investor may not be experienced with rent to own and the contracts may be amateurish or incomplete.

Another issue is that there likely won't be a realtor involved and therefore it may be difficult to know what the true fair market value of the house is.

Third, because you didn't actually choose the house, you may not actually love the house, and you end buying the house more out of convenience or fear that this may by your only chance to own your own home. If you can't see yourself living in the house for at least five years, you probably shouldn't buy it.

Also, you have to ask yourself why the owner is offering a rent-to-own instead of selling the house the traditional way. Maybe there are problems with the house you are not aware of or maybe the owners know there are expensive repairs coming up in the near future, and they want to offload their problem onto you.

An investor may try to rush the process as "time is money" in the fix and flip business. Make sure you take the time to get a proper appraisal and inspection. You may be tempted not to. After all, you have been living in the house you should know what the state of the house is. But, do you know when the furnace, hot water heater or roof will need to be replaced? These things all have a known life expectancy and should be replaced when or soon after that life expectancy is up. Always get a home inspection so that there are no nasty surprises.

House First Rent-to-Own puts the seller first, and your interests are really secondary to the seller's. Because you are not really in control of the process, this puts you at increased risk of getting a substandard home or even getting outright scammed.

2. Tenant First Rent-to-Own.

Tenant first rent to own is a somewhat newer way to do rent-to-own and, in my opinion, is the best and safest way to create a Win-Win situation for everyone involved, especially the Tenant/Buyer.

In this scenario, you contact and apply to an experienced rent-to-own company that will be knowledgeable and professional in the rent-to-own process. You will work with a team of professionals, including your rent-to-own professional, a mortgage specialist, a realtor, a real estate lawyer and a professional home inspector. They will also have access to a good contractor and connections with other building trades, if necessary.

Once you are approved for the program, you with the help of your realtor will get to choose any home within your pre-approved price range in your desired market. Your realtor and rent-to-own professional will help ensure you are getting a good home, in your price range, which is also a good investment for you in the future. They'll make sure it is in a good location, in a good neighborhood and is likely to appreciate at or above the market average over time. The real estate lawyer will ensure that all contracts are complete and legal.

This process really puts the tenant buyer first and is the best way to ensure that the process is Win-Win for everyone involved.

If you are currently renting, you may ask, "Why should I even try to own my own home? It sounds expensive, complicated and I don't really see the advantage of owning a house."

In the next chapter we will talk about 12 advantages of owning your own home.

Chapter Two:

Twelve Advantages of Home Ownership over Renting

"Try imagining a place where it's always safe and warm."
"Come in," she said.
"I'll give ya shelter from the storm."
-- Bob Dylan

Everyone needs shelter. Shelter is considered one of life's three essentials: food, water and shelter. Unless you plan on living on the streets, in a homeless shelter or couch surfing at a friend's house for the rest of your life, eventually you're going to have to pay for shelter. You probably already are. Obviously most people don't choose one of these first three choices, so you can either rent your shelter or you can own it.

Let's think about renting for a moment. Renting is great for things that you need only occasionally. For example, if you only ski one or two times per year, renting your equipment is far more economical than buying a full set of ski equipment, keeping it maintained and storing it for the other three hundred and sixty three days of the year. On the other hand, if skiing is a passion of yours and you ski even five or ten days per year, over a few years it is cheaper, not to mention far more convenient, to own your own equipment. Most things that you use every day you would never consider renting such as clothes, your vehicle, your kitchen utensils et cetera. But people continue to rent their shelter year after year, probably because they don't think they can afford to buy. I think people can't afford NOT to buy and I'll show you why throughout the rest of this chapter.

Is home ownership the right choice for everyone? No. But here are twelve reasons why homeownership may be right for you.

Advantage #1: Build Equity Every Month

Let's start by talking about equity. The word equity means "evenness" or "fairness," but when we talk about equity in real estate we really mean home equity. Home equity is the difference between the Fair Market Value of a home (what you can sell it for) and the unpaid mortgage balance on the home. For example, if you have a home that could sell for $300,000 and you have a mortgage balance of $210,000, then you have $90,000 in equity or 30 percent equity in the home.

$300,000 - $210,000 = $90,000

$90,000 / $300,000 X 100% = 30%

Equity is the "holy grail" of real estate. Home equity is built up in two ways. As you make your mortgage payments every month, your equity slowly builds up. We call this "mortgage pay down." Your mortgage payment is made up of two parts, Principal and Interest. The Principal is the amount your mortgage is paid down and adds to your equity. The Interest is your cost of borrowing and becomes the bank's profit. The banks didn't lend you all that money out of the goodness of their hearts; they take their profit in interest payments. Thankfully, in 2016 lending rates are at an all-time low and hopefully will remain that way for at least a few more years.

The second way to build equity is appreciation. We will talk about appreciation in the next section. (Advantage #2).

Advantage #2: Real Estate is an Appreciating Asset

"Appreciation is a wonderful thing: It makes what is excellent in others belong to us as well."
-- Voltaire.

On average, the price of real estate goes up, or appreciates, at 3-4 percent per year across Canada and the United States. In some markets, like Vancouver and Toronto in 2015 and 2016 when this book was written, appreciation can be much higher, up to 20 percent per year in some cases. Just ask your grandparents or anyone over the age of 65 what they paid for their first home (maybe less than you paid for your first car!) and you will get a sense of how much real estate appreciates over time.

Appreciation is quite unique to real estate. Buy a new car, new bike, or article of new clothing, and drive, ride, or wear it once and it is now worth approximately one third to one half or what you paid for it. These are called depreciating assets. Not with real estate; while it doesn't appreciate every year, on average it will appreciate almost like clockwork. Your rent payment will likely go up every year too, but you probably don't appreciate that! I call the appreciation we've been talking about "passive appreciation."

If you keep your house in good repair and update a few things now and then, you can expect to realize this passive appreciation. If the $300,000 house in our example were to appreciate at 3 percent per year, after one year the house would be worth $309,000 and after five years $348,000.

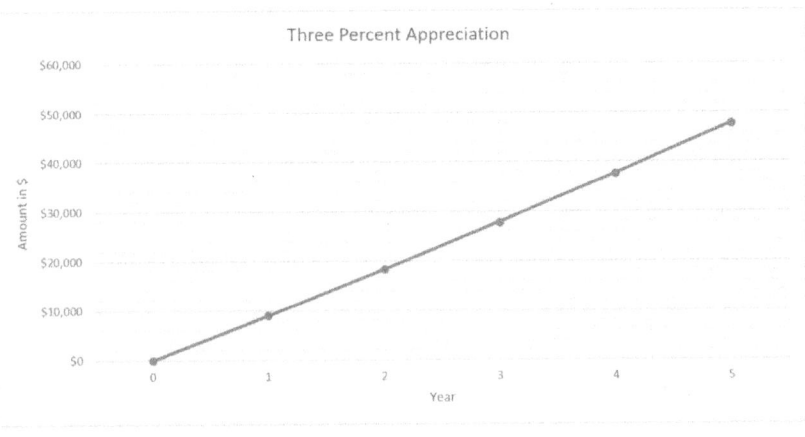

There's a second kind of appreciation called "forced appreciation" or "active appreciation." There are many ways to force appreciation of your home. Some of the more common ways would be to renovate the kitchen or bathrooms of the home, paint the interior or exterior of the home with fresh, contemporary paint colors, add a rental suite, add an enclosed garage, or even put in new landscaping. These all increase the value of the home above and beyond the normal passive appreciation. Taking advantage of appreciation and building equity has huge advantages that we'll talk about later.

Advantage #3: Your Home Appreciates Tax Free

"In this world nothing can be said to be certain, except death and taxes."
-- Benjamin Franklin 1789

Ben Franklin was mostly right about death and taxes, but there are a few exceptions. When you go to work, you pay income taxes. If you save and invest your money, you pay capital gains tax on any money that you make. Even when you die, you may have to pay estate taxes. Death and taxes on the same day, how's that for a kick in the pants!

But there are very few ways to make money without paying taxes. One way is the relatively new tax-free savings account (TFSA) (or Roth IRA in America). If you manage to save up some money after paying your income taxes, you can put that money into a TFSA or Roth IRA, invest it, and any money you make is tax free.

You can defer paying income tax by putting your money into an RRSP (or 401K) and investing it there. You get a tax deduction for the year that you contribute, then you pay income tax on the money once you take it out of the RRSP after retirement. The tax is deferred, but certainly not tax free.

The appreciation in your home, however, is tax free. If you buy a house for $300,000.00 and sell it five years later for $348,000 (just a little over 3 percent appreciation per year) you get to keep that extra $48,000 tax free! There is no other investment that I know of where you make that kind of money and keep it tax free.

Advantage #4: The Pride and Freedom of Ownership

"The American Dream is one of success, home ownership, college education for one's children, and having a secure job to provide these and other goals."
--Leonard Boswell

When you finally achieve your dream of home ownership it's a monumental achievement and a source of great pride, especially if you've had some financial difficulty on the road to ownership. You are now the king and/or the queen of your own castle! No one can tell you that you have to move. No one can increase your rent. You can turn up the music (within reason) or buy that electric guitar or a drum kit you've always dreamed of. If the dishwasher breaks down or there is a leaky faucet you can choose to fix it yourself or get someone in right away to repair it. No asking permission. No waiting days or weeks for the landlord to approve and then arrange for the repairs.

You have achieved a degree of financial success that not everyone attains and is becoming more and more difficult to achieve.

When you own your home you take pride in its appearance and keeping it in good working order. Let's face it, when you're a renter, even if you're a great tenant and a bit of a neat freak you're going to do the minimum required to keep the place up to your standards. If the paint is a little drab or marked up, you'll put a picture over it. If the window coverings are a little dated, well too bad. It's a whole different story when you actually own your own home. You don't like the paint in the living room? You can paint it the exact color that you want. You don't have to ask permission you don't have to get the color approved. You can paint it with pink polka dots if you want and no one can stop you, except maybe your spouse. Over time you can transform your home into exactly the way you want it and be confident that you are increasing the value of the home and building your equity.

Advantage #5: Forced Savings

"I'm thankful for the three ounce Ziploc bag, so that I can have somewhere to put my savings."
-- Paula Poundstone

Let's be honest. Saving money is difficult and most of us are not saving enough. Owning your own home is like a forced savings plan. Let's assume you're currently renting. How did your landlord decide on what the rent was going to be? If they are sophisticated investors they calculated how much it cost to pay the principal and interest of the mortgage, plus the property tax, plus the cost of home insurance, and then added as much as they thought they could get on top as monthly cash flow.

The rent that you are paying now is paying down the principle (building equity) on the mortgage, which amounts to a savings program for your landlord, but using your money.

When you own your own home, that principle pay down builds your equity and is essentially a forced savings plan for you. Over just a few years that can add up to a lot of money.

On a $300,000 home let's assume your mortgage Principle plus Interest plus Property taxes plus Insurance (sometimes called your PITI payment) costs approximately $1,350 per month. Approximately $470 of that payment is the principle payment. Over the course of one year that's over $5,640. Over five years this adds up to over $28,000! Right now this is going into your landlord's pocket instead of yours. Just think what you could do with an extra $28,000. Don't forget about the $48,000 you would expect to make from appreciation. That's over $76,000 you would have in equity after only five years.

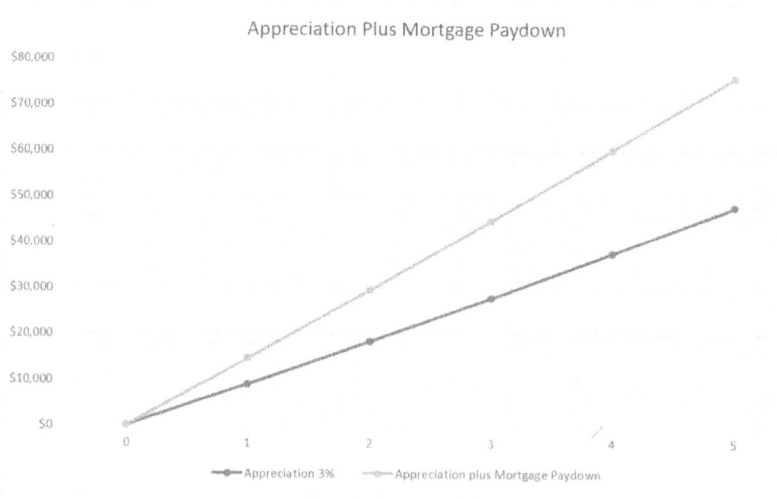

Advantage #6: Leveragability

"Business, that's easily defined - It's other people's money."
--Peter Drucker

There are multiple forms of leverage that open up to you when you own your own home. We will talk about two big ones here.

The first form of leverage is what people in real estate call using OPM or "Other People's Money."

Let's put your investor's cap on for a moment. If you think about the home you want to buy purely as an investment, you are using OPM (i.e. the bank's money) to pay for most of the house.

Let's say you buy that house for $300,000 with a ten percent down payment. Your down payment would be $30,000 but you would now control a $300,000 investment. Let's compare this to investing your $30,000 dollars in the stock market and I think you will see that leverage can be a huge advantage.

Earlier we said that real estate appreciates at approximately 3-4 percent per year on average. Let's assume you bought your home for $300,000 and after one year it appreciated only 3 percent. Three percent of $300,000 is $9,000 so your house is now worth $309,000. That's $9,000 of equity that you have built up. But you didn't invest $300,000, you only invested $30,000. So the $9,000 that you made is actually a 30 percent Return on Investment (ROI)!

$9000/ $30,000 X 100% = 30% ROI.

Remember from Advantage #2 that we calculated appreciation on your $300,000 house over 5 years to be $48,000. The return on your $30,000 investment is actually 160 percent in 5 years!

$48,000/ $30,000 X 100% = 160% ROI in five years.

Now let's go back and look at how you would do in the stock market. The average return of the Dow Jones Industrial over the last 20 years has been about 6 percent, or about 8.5percent if you reinvested all your dividends. In one year, your $30,000 in the stock market would now be worth $32,550 for a total profit of $2,550. Not bad at all, but I would still rather have $9,000 from my real estate investment.

$2550/ $30,000 X 100% = 8.5% ROI.

What your banker or broker doesn't tell you is that the 8.5 percent return is before the fees have been applied. Most mutual funds that you would buy would have fees of between 1 percent and 3 percent per year. That reduces your 8.5percent return to say 6.5 percent.

6.5%/ 100% X $30,000 = $1,950 ROI per year

Over 5 years at an 8.5 percent return, your return on investment would be $15,110.

$15,110/ $30,000 X 100% = 50.4% ROI after 5 years

Once the fees have been applied, however, your return is reduced to approximately $11,100.

$11,100/$30,000 X 100% = 37% ROI after 5 years

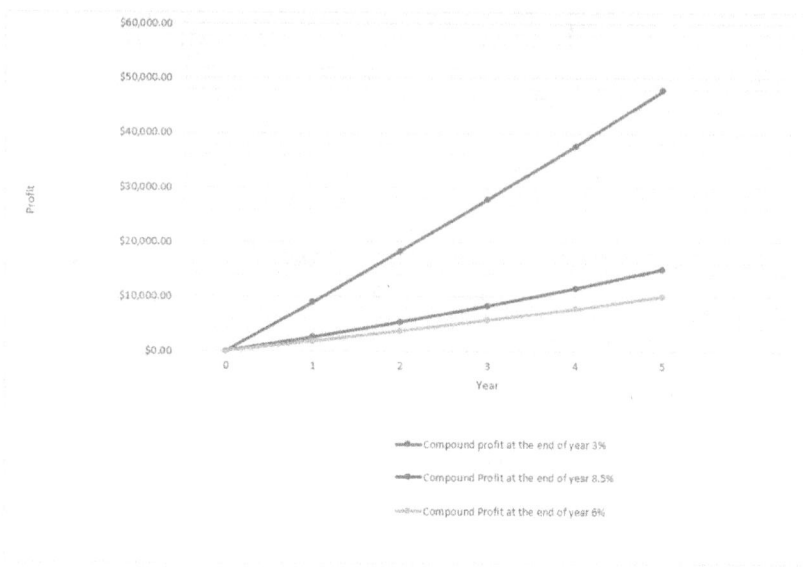

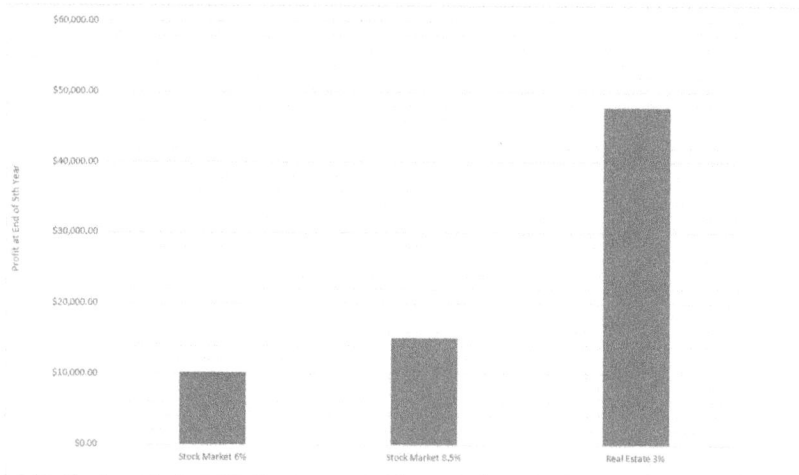

I think you can see that using the leverage of other's people money can greatly increase your return on investment. In this example, your return on investment over 5 years from owning your own home was 160 percent versus 54 percent or actually 37 percent after the fees have been applied to your stock market investments.

Now let's talk about the second way to use leverage. As your equity in your home increases (by a combination of appreciation and mortgage pay down), you can use that equity to get a home equity line of credit (HELOC). The money that you now have available in your HELOC can be used for anything that you choose. For example, you could use the money to:

Make improvements to your home to further force appreciation.

You can use the money to invest in yourself by increasing your education or invest in the education of your children. You can even use the money to invest in something that you think will have a nice rate of return.

Of course this money is not free. The bank will charge you interest on any money that you remove from your line of credit. We will talk more about this in Advantage #7 (Borrowing Power).

Advantage #7: Borrowing Power

"I would borrow money all day long, if the cost of borrowing is less than the expected return."
--Brad Schneider

"You cannot keep borrowing more and more and keep spending more and more without eventually having a day of reckoning." **--Wilbur Ross**

When you own your own home, you instantly have more borrowing power.

Home ownership gives you more credibility with the banks and other lenders, even if you don't have a lot of equity in your home. In the bank's view, you are a better credit risk. You are less likely to quit your job or do something to get yourself fired. You have committed to stay in the community that you have bought into, and you are mature enough to see the value of owning a home. With increased credibility comes increased borrowing power, making it much easier to:

Buy a new car.

Borrow to start a new business or upgrade a business you already own.

Go back to school or upgrade your work skills.

Pay for post-secondary school for yourself or your kids.

In addition to this instant borrowing power, over time you will be able to tap into the equity you have built up and borrow against this equity. We talked about equity in Advantage #1. Borrowing against your equity is part of the leveragability that we talked about in Advantage #6.

There are three main ways to tap into the equity of your home:

1. Remortgage

At any time during your mortgage, you have the option to remortgage your home. Most banks will allow you to withdraw up to 80 percent of your home's value as equity. You may also be able to reset your amortization back to 25 or 30 years. This allows you to withdraw a large amount of the equity of your home. Advantages of remortgaging are that you will usually be able to get the best fixed or variable rates that your bank can offer. Also, if interest rates have gone down, when you remortgage your monthly payments will now use that new lower interest rate. On the other hand, if interest rates have gone up, you may have to pay a higher interest rate. Also, your bank will charge you a penalty for breaking your original mortgage. This is usually three months interest but can be higher, and you should check your mortgage carefully before considering remortgaging.

2. Second mortgage

A second mortgage, sometimes called a home equity loan, is when a bank or lending company places a second mortgage on your home, and you get to withdraw the amount of money of that second mortgage. The advantage of a second mortgage over remortgaging is that there is no penalty to be paid. However, the interest rate is usually higher, sometimes up to 10-15 percent, and there are usually additional fees charged to set up the mortgage. Each month you pay your original mortgage payment plus the new second mortgage payment.

3. Home equity line of credit

A home equity line of credit (HELOC) is a relatively new way to access the equity of your home. The bank again may allow you to go up to 75 or 80 percent of the equity in your home and remove that equity to be used as you choose. Usually you will pay a variable interest rate, which can go up or go down as interest rates change, plus a small premium, often 1 percent or 2 percent above prime rate. One advantage of a HELOC is that your monthly payment is interest only. Also, you only pay interest on the money that you have withdrawn. An additional advantage is that money that you have paid back into the line of credit can be accessed again in the future. The home equity line of credit is a great, flexible way to access the equity in your home and is likely the preferred method over remortgaging or a second mortgage.

A Word of Caution: A HELOC, remortgage or second mortgage MUST be used responsibly. The bank uses your home as collateral. If you get yourself over your head in debt and can't pay your mortgage as well as the interest on your line of credit, the bank may be forced to foreclose on your home and you could lose all of that equity you worked so hard to build up.

Advantage #8: Cost Certainty

One advantage of home ownership is that you can have cost certainty if you want it.

Mortgages come in two basic forms: fixed and variable rate mortgages.

Fixed Rate Mortgage:

With a fixed rate mortgage your interest rate is set at the beginning and won't change until it is time to renew your mortgage, often 5 or even 10 years later. This means that your monthly mortgage payment will not change during the term. This can give you peace of mind that you have your expenses control.

Variable Rate Mortgage:

With a variable rate mortgage the interest rate that you pay to borrow goes up or down as your bank raises or lowers its prime interest rate (usually based on the Bank of Canada or Federal Reserve rate). This means that your monthly mortgage payment could go up (or down) making it difficult to keep an accurate budget.

You may ask, if a fixed rate mortgage gives you cost certainty, why would anyone choose a variable rate mortgage? Usually the variable rate will be a little lower than the fixed rate, so there is some savings, at least initially, with a variable mortgage. That means with a fixed rate mortgage you pay a small price for the cost certainty.

There's also something called a blended mortgage which is half fixed and half variable. This gives you the best (and worst) of both worlds and will have an overall interest rate somewhere between the fixed and variable rate. You can also "lock in" your variable rate mortgage at any time if you think interest rates are going to rise significantly.

Talk to your mortgage specialist for more details to help you decide which option is best for you.

Advantage #9: Your Home Can Make You Money

Did you know that owning your own home can actually make you money? You just have to be a little creative and flexible. Here are several ways you can make money from the house you own:

Rent out a bedroom. This could be a traditional roommate, a foreign exchange student, or even billeting a student athlete who has traveled to play for a local sports team.

A self-contained rental suite (sometimes called a mortgage helper). A rental suite gives you extra cash each month to help with your monthly bills and can help you pay down your mortgage faster, saving you a lot of money in interest payments. If you put (a legal) suite in a home you already own, you will dramatically increase the value of the home (i.e. Forced Appreciation).

A coach house. Some houses have a coach house in the back that can be rented out too. Some cities will allow you to build a coach house on your property to increase the amount of rental housing in the area. With small, prefabricated homes becoming better and cheaper all the time, this can be a viable option depending on where you live and how much space there is behind your house.

Rent out your house while you're away. This used to be much more complicated and it was difficult to find a renter for a short term rental. With companies like airbnb, it is extremely easy and lucrative to rent out your house for a short term rental. Just make sure that short term rentals are allowed where you live.

Rent out a parking spot. If you live in an area where parking is difficult to find, you may be able to rent out a spot in your garage or even a spot in your carport to someone who lives or works nearby.

Rent out storage space in your basement or garage.

Rent your house out as a TV, commercial or a movie set. If there is a movie being filmed in your area, these film companies are often looking for set locations and will pay a high price to rent your house.

As you can see, there are many ways you can make money when you own your own home. These examples just scratch the surface. You just have to be flexible and get a little creative.

Advantage #10: Retire Comfortably

Many people look forward to retirement their whole working lives, but the "golden years" of retirement may not be so "golden" if you don't have enough money to enjoy it, let alone cover increasing health care costs as we age. People are living longer, saving less, borrowing more, and the days of jobs with good pension packages are quickly vanishing. All these factors put people at serious risk of running out of money when they should be trying to enjoy retirement.

Now imagine that you have always been a renter. Each year your rent goes up a little bit, but you are on a fixed (and relatively low) income. You could be in a serious financial bind.

If you own your home, even if it's not fully paid off, you have a much better chance of enjoying retirement with enough money.

There are three main options to help with your retirement:

1. Downsize

If you want to stay in the same community, maybe to remain near friends or family, you can simply downsize. Moving to a smaller home, townhouse, duplex or condo can free up a large amount of that equity you have built up over the years, still allowing you to spend time with the family and friends that you love.

2. Move to a less expensive community

Especially if you live in or near a bigger town or city, you can often move to a nice community farther from the city center for far less money, but still be close enough to drive to the city occasionally if there's an event you want to attend. Or, if you are really adventurous, you could move to another country with a much lower cost of living and live like "royalty."

3. Reverse mortgage

A third option, if you want to continue living in your same home in the same community is to take out a reverse mortgage.

If you are a homeowner over the age of 55, you can get up to 50 percent of your home's value through a reverse mortgage. You don't have to repay the reverse mortgage until you sell your home or pass away.

By using the equity you have built up in your home in one of these three ways you can:

Invest the money to increase your savings for later in retirement.

Use the money to augment your retirement income if you are on a low, fixed income.

Use the money to help out family members now instead of waiting until you pass away and passing down money through an inheritance.

Advantage #11: Build Generational Wealth

I realize that if you are struggling to buy your first home, that what you are going to pass down through inheritance is probably one of the last things on your mind, but it is an important idea nonetheless.

If you are able to buy a house and pay it off during your working years, even if you spend every cent you have during your retirement, when you pass away you will be able to give your family members a big financial boost. This is one way families become a little wealthier from generation to generation. Don't we all want our kids to have it a little easier or be a little better off than we are? You would have to save a lot of money to have the same impact as owning your home and letting time and appreciation turn that home into a very valuable asset.

Advantage #12: Tax Incentives

In the United States your mortgage interest and property tax are tax deductible. This can result in a large tax break that renters do not get. Unfortunately, in Canada mortgage interest and property tax are not tax deductible.

Bonus Reason: Renting is great for your landlord, but sucks for you. When you rent, your landlord is getting all the benefits we just talked about, but they are using your money to get those benefits. They aren't bad people, they just know a good deal when they see one. You have a roof over your head but you are paying dearly for it and get none of the amazing benefits of home ownership.

Chapter Three:

Disadvantages of Home Ownership

Home ownership is not for everyone, at least not at any given time. You have to have a consistent, steady income and be committed to the community you are buying into. Here are some disadvantages of home ownership over renting.

1. Long term financial commitment.

You lose the flexibility to move around when you own a home. You also need to ensure you have steady income to cover your monthly mortgage payment. If you are likely to be transferred or laid off from your job in the near future, you should probably rent until things become more stable.

2. You are responsible for all maintenance and repair costs.

Enough said.

3. Higher up-front costs.

What is the true cost of home ownership? If you're like most first time home buyers, your answer would likely be "whatever the purchase price of the house is." In our example, $300,000. This is not the true cost of ownership. First of all, you probably don't have $300,000 to pay cash for your house, so you are going to have to get a mortgage from a bank or a credit union.

In reality, the true cost of home ownership is a combination of two distinct categories of costs. These are:

A. The cost to buy the house.
B. The ongoing monthly costs.

A. Cost to Buy the House

Down payment plus Closing Costs. To buy a house you have to pay an initial down payment to the bank, usually between five to twenty percent of the purchase price. Then there are a number of other costs called closing costs. These are listed here with a rough estimate of the cost.

An appraisal. Required by the bank to determine the true value of the house - $250.

A home inspection - $400.

Lawyer or notary fees - $1,200.

Land transfer tax – Variable depending on where you live. – In British Columbia, $4,000 in our $300,000 house example.

Mortgage default insurance or CMHC fees - $6,480 with 10 percent down payment on our $300,000 house. The bank will usually add this to the mortgage so you don't have to pay this up front, but increases the size of the mortgage.

So with a 10 percent down payment of $30,000 plus $5,850 ($12,330 - $6480) in closing costs, the initial cost of buying versus renting is $35,850.

B. Monthly Cost of Ownership (PITI payments)

These costs will vary depending on where you live and what interest rate you are paying on your mortgage. These numbers are just a rough example for a $300,000 in British Columbia:

Principal - $470

Interest - $605

Property taxes - $190

Home insurance - $100

So monthly costs, not including maintenance and repair, would be approximately $1,365. This may be higher or lower than what you would pay to rent the same house.

4. Risk of Foreclosure.

If for some reason you cannot make your mortgage payment, whether that is because of job loss, injury, divorce or some other reason, you could be at risk of either having to sell your house quickly (possibly at a loss) or having the bank foreclose on your mortgage. In foreclosure you would lose all of the equity you have built up and badly damage your credit rating making it much more difficult to qualify for another mortgage or other financing in the future.

Chapter Four:

The Rent to Own Process in a Nutshell

The process of rent to own can seem confusing and intimidating until you understand each of the steps involved and understand some new terminology that you may not have heard of before.

In this chapter I will briefly outline each of the 15 steps of the rent to own process. Yes, I said 15 steps. That's one reason you need to work with an experienced rent-to-own company. Bear with me, it's not as complicated as it sounds.

I will also explain some of the new terminology.

We will go into further detail for each of the steps in Chapter Eight.

First some definitions:

Tenant Buyer – The person or people entering into a rent-to-own deal to become homeowners in a few short years.

Rent-to-own Specialist – Could be an individual investor or a company that specializes in rent-to-own as a means to help the Tenant Buyer get out of the rental cycle and become a home owner.

Initial Option Credit – The money that you will need to put down at beginning of the rent-to-own process. This is returned to you at the end of the program to go towards your down payment for your own mortgage.

Monthly Option Credit – Money paid each month, on top of your rent payment. This accumulates over the term of the program to achieve a 10 percent down payment plus closing costs by the end of the program.

Now back to those 15 steps in the rent-to-own process.

1. Pick a rent to own company to work with. The most important thing when picking a rent-to-own company is to find one that has lots of experience and preferably specializes in the rent to own process.

2. Submit an application to the rent-to-own company. This can often be done online or the company may have an application you can download and email back.

3. Initial interview. Most companies will have an initial interview. This interview may be face to face or less likely by telephone. Some companies now can use Skype or Face Time to have an initial interview with out of town clients.

4. Initial approval. After your application has been filled out and following the initial interview, you hopefully will receive initial approval.

5. Meet with the mortgage broker. This is the step where the rent-to-own company will decide whether you are a good fit financially for their rent-to-own program. You will be asked for documents confirming your income, your work history, how much money you have saved for an initial down payment and you will be required to consent to or provide a current credit bureau report.

6. Final approval. If you receive final approval, this means that the rent-to-own company believes that you have a very good chance of completing the program and becoming a homeowner in just a few short years. If for some reason you are not approved, the company will often tell you the exact steps you need to take to get final approval and they will likely invite you to reapply in the future once those steps have been taken.

7. Meet with the realtor. This is where the program gets exciting. You get to meet with the realtor and tell them exactly the type of house you are looking for, including the number of bedrooms and bathrooms you want, whether you need a yard and enclosed garage et cetera. The realtor will take this information and begin to show you houses that meet your criteria and that fit within the budget for which you have been approved.

8. Sign two contracts. There are actually a number of contracts you will sign but there are two main contracts. The first contract is just a standard Lease or Rental contract. The second contract is what is called an Option Contract. This gives you the option to buy the house and sets the final purchase price that you will pay at the end of the program.

9. The rent-to-own company or an outside investor buys the house that you choose. Because you do not qualify for bank financing at this time, in order to get into the house of your

choice, either the rent-to-own company or an outside investor buys the house for you and rents the house to you as you go through the program and ultimately qualify for your own financing.

10. Pay an Initial Option Credit. The initial option credit is similar to a down payment you would have to pay when getting a mortgage for a house. The difference is that the initial option credit will be lower than the down payment required, usually 3-5 percent of the purchase price. The initial option credit is returned to you at the end of the program and acts as part of your true down payment when you purchase the house.

11. Move into your future home!

12. Pay your monthly rent payment and a Monthly Option Credit for the length of your contract, usually 3 years. The rent you will pay will be the fair market rent for the house that you choose and the Monthly Option Credit will be calculated to ensure that you accumulate a good down payment as well as closing costs by the completion of the rent-to-own program.

13. Maintain your future home as if it were your own. Because you are moving into the home that you will own in a few short years, you will want to maintain your home to make sure that it maintains as much value and appreciation as possible.

14. Follow strict instructions on how to repair or build your credit rating. This is a huge advantage of a rent-to-own program. A mortgage broker or credit repair specialist will give you the exact steps required to improve your credit rating so that you can qualify for a mortgage at the end of the program as well as pay the lowest interest rate possible.

15. Buy the house from the investor. At the end of the program you should be able to easily qualify for your own mortgage through the accumulation of your Option Credits as well as the credit repair process. In this final step, you truly become a home owner and finally realize your dream of home ownership!

We will go over each of these steps in further detail in Chapter Eight.

Chapter Five:

Who is a Good Candidate for Rent-to-Own?

Rent-to-Own is a great strategy for anyone who, for whatever reason, can't qualify for bank financing at this time, but wants to finally own their own home. The typical person is someone who values home ownership and is willing to dedicate themselves to the program of rent-to-own. The program works but the steps must be followed exactly as laid out. Below are the four most common reasons why someone may not qualify for bank financing and therefore may consider rent-to-own as a solution.

1. People who have a small down payment. Depending on your financial situation, banks or mortgage companies may require between 5 percent and even up to 20 percent for a down payment on a home. As we all know saving is difficult and if housing prices keep increasing in your area it can be very difficult to save enough money to qualify.

2. People with no credit history. The credit rating companies such as Equifax or TransUnion use your credit history to assign a credit score to you. The banks use this credit score to determine how risky it is to lend money to you and what your chances of defaulting on the loan or mortgage are. If you are new to the country you may not have enough credit history for the credit companies to assign you a credit score. Another common scenario is someone who is recently divorced. If you have joint accounts and joint credit cards, often these only count as credit history for one of the partners, typically the primary card holder. Another less common scenario is someone who doesn't believe in buying on credit. You may never have owned a credit card or are in the habit of paying cash for all your purchases. This is a fantastic attribute and very financially responsible. Unfortunately, the credit companies don't have enough data to assign you a credit score. Banks generally want to see at least three years of credit history to approve a mortgage.

3. People with bruised credit. If you have a number of late payments reported on your credit report, if you've had an account sent to a collection agency or if you have had a previous foreclosure or bankruptcy in your past, your credit rating will suffer accordingly. Job loss, divorce, difficult to pay student loans are common reasons for missed payments. Unfortunately, sometimes people even develop a poor credit rating by being a little naïve. They fully intend to pay their Visa bill or cell phone bill but don't realize the importance of paying that bill before the due date. Any late payments that you make get reported on your credit report and remain there for a minimum of seven years.

4. People who are self-employed. For some reason the banks consider self-employed people to be an increased risk, even though these people are often the hardest working and most reliable people you could find. The banks generally require three years of stated income to qualify for a mortgage. Unfortunately most self-employed people pay themselves only a small salary and keep as much of their income inside the business to help the business grow and to take advantage of corporate tax benefits. Most banks won't take this into account and only consider the small income that you paid yourself despite the fact that you may have considerable assets within the corporation. This may require a self-employed person to pay themselves a higher income resulting in higher income taxes for a period of three years to satisfy the bank's lending criteria.

Chapter Six:

Twelve Benefits of Rent-to-Own for the Tenant Buyer

There are many benefits of rent-to-own to the tenant buyer. Here are 12 benefits that you get to take advantage of as the tenant buyer in a rent-to-own program.

1. You get immediate control and possession of the property of your choice. That's right, you choose any house on market. Once you have chosen your house, you get to move in right away and will never be forced to move again until you choose to. Nobody likes moving. It is time consuming, expensive, and exhausting. It is a wonderful feeling when you are moving into your home and may never have to move again.

2. You become a homeowner in training. The monthly rent that you will pay during the program will closely approximate the true cost of home ownership. Your rent will cover the cost of the Principal and Interest of the mortgage as well as the property Taxes and Insurance of the home (your PITI payments). Fair market rent means you cover these costs plus a small amount of monthly profit for the landlord, in this case the investor that has bought the house for you. Another way in which you become a homeowner in training is that you will be responsible for routine maintenance and repairs of the house during the program. For example, you will have to change the filters on the furnace, learn to turn the outside faucets off in the winter if necessary, etc.

3. The Initial Option Credit (IOC) is lower than a standard down payment. Depending on the program, you will have to pay an Initial Option Credit, which may be a percentage of the house price or may be a fixed amount such as $10,000. The Initial Option Credit will be lower than the down payment that would be required to buy the home. The IOC is returned back to you and go towards the down payment at the end of the program.

4. There is no obligation to buy the house. You have the right or option to buy the house at the end of the program but no obligation. This means that if your circumstances change and for some reason you can't or don't want to buy the house, you get to walk away at the end of the program with no legal obligation to buy the house. This means that no one will try to sue you if you don't buy the house at the end of the program.

5. Cost certainty. The rental payments that you will pay are fixed for the term of the contract, usually three years. That's right, your rent will not go up for the entire term of the contract. No New Year's rent increase surprise!

6. The future purchase price is predetermined. This is another form of cost certainty. At the beginning of the program, the final purchase price of the house will be determined, usually by applying a set percentage for appreciation which is added to the initial purchase price of the house. This is another form of cost certainty. Even if house prices appreciate much more than the calculated appreciation, the future purchase price remains the same and you benefit from the additional appreciation.

7. You benefit financially from any improvements made to the property. During the term of the program, if you make any improvements to the house such as repainting the interior, putting in new flooring, or renovating the kitchen or the bathroom, you will directly benefit from the added appreciation to the house. Just remember that the term of the rent-to-own process is not a time to be taking on large expenses as you are meant to be saving for your down payment and closing costs for the final purchase of your home.

8. Your credit rating improves. Through good credit counseling from the mortgage broker or credit counselor that you work with during the program, your credit rating should steadily improve over the rent-to-own process. This not only allows you to qualify for the mortgage but also allows you to qualify for lower interest rates on your mortgage or any other future purchases such as a new car.

9. Allows more time to accumulate a larger down payment. The larger the down payment that you have when you make the final purchase of your home the better.

First of all, a larger down payment will lower your monthly mortgage payments making it a little easier to cover your bills each month.

Secondly a larger down payment saves on CMHC fees. For what banks call a "conventional mortgage," a 20 percent down payment is needed and no CMHC fees are required. A first time homebuyer can often pay as little as 5 or 10 percent as a down payment on their first home. This is called a "high ratio mortgage." This sounds great, but the banks will require you to take out mortgage default insurance from a company such as CMHC (Canadian Mortgage Housing Corporation). The closer you can get to the 20 percent down payment when you make the final purchase of your home, the lower the CMHC fee. The CMHC fee is calculated as a percentage of the purchase price and can be as high as 3.6 percent if you pay only 5 percent as a down payment. For our example of a $300,000 house that's an additional $10,260 in CMHC fees. The CMHC fee for a 10 percent down payment is 2.40 percent and a 15 percent down payment is 1.8 percent or only $6,480 and $4,590 respectively.

$300,000 x 0.95 = $285,000 x 3.6% = $10,260

$300,000 x 0.90 = $270,000 x 2.4% = $6,480

$300,000 x 0.85 = $255,000 x 1.8% = $4,590

This mortgage insurance is purely for the bank's benefit, not yours, but you get the privilege of paying for it.

10. The rent-to-own program ensures that you have enough funds for a down payment plus the closing costs. Through the Initial Option Credit plus the Monthly Option Credit, the program will ensure that you have 10 to 12 percent of the purchase price saved up for a down payment plus the closing costs. Many people do not consider the closing costs when they buy a home, especially if they are buying their first home. These closing costs were discussed in Chapter Three and can add up quickly and put a serious dent into the money you have saved for you down payment. A good rent-to-own company will ensure that you have the 10 to 12 percent for your down payment and your closing costs.

11. Enables accurate budgeting of household finances. Part of becoming more financially responsible is learning to make a budget for your household finances and sticking within that budget. Because you monthly rental payment closely approximates the true monthly cost of home ownership, you will be able to come up with an accurate budget. In addition to the usual monthly costs of your mortgage payment, property taxes and insurance, it is a good idea to budget for the costs of routine maintenance on your home as well as having money set aside for any unexpected expenses such as repair or replacement of appliances should they break down. It's always a good idea to know the age of the roof on your house as most roofs have an expected life span. If your roof needs to be replaced in the next 5 to 10 years, it may be a good idea to start putting money aside now so that you are not burdened by a large payment in the future.

12. Lower closing costs. We talked about closing costs in Chapter Three as well as in Section 10 above. By a stroke of good luck, the way that rent-to-own works will likely lower your closing costs.

You will never have to pay realtor's fees. When the investor initially buys the house from the seller, it is the seller's responsibility to pay the realtors fees. Because you are going to buy the house directly from the investor, no realtor is necessary and therefore no realtor fees need to be paid.

You may also save on inspection fees. Inspection fees are usually around $400. Because an inspection was done on your house at the beginning of the program and because you have lived in the house since that time, you may feel that it is not necessary to obtain a new inspection.

If you use a mortgage broker to help you obtain your mortgage, their fee is paid by the bank.

We already talked about lower interest rates as your credit rating improves and lower CMHC fees with a higher down payment.

These are just 12 of the benefits to the tenant buyer in a typical rent-to-own program. There's no such thing as a free lunch as they say so of course there are some disadvantages of rent-to-own. We will talk further about these in Chapter Seven.

Chapter Seven:

Disadvantages of Rent-to-Own

While I believe that rent-to-own is the cheapest, fastest and easiest way for people to achieve their dream of home ownership, there are some small disadvantages that you need to be aware of.

1. You have to have at least a small amount of money saved up.

To enter a rent-to-own program, you have to have at least some money saved up. All programs will require an Initial Option Credit, as we discussed in Chapter Four. The rent-to-own company, as well as the investor, will want to know that you have some "skin in the game". This shows that you are committed to the program and also shows that you are responsible enough to move toward the future down payment of your home. Obviously, if you choose to continue renting, this initial payment is not necessary.

2. Your monthly payments will be higher.

Each month you will be required to pay your monthly rent as well as the Monthly Option Credit. This means that the overall monthly payment will be higher than if you continued renting. The Monthly Option Credit allows you to accumulate the money that you will need for your down payment when you finally purchase the house. My opinion is that this is not really a disadvantage, but is a forced savings program that allows you to purchase your home as quickly as possible.

3. More responsibility.

The tenant-buyer is responsible for all routine maintenance and repairs during the program. This is part of being a "homeowner in training" that we talked about in Chapter Seven. This means that you are responsible for maintaining your house and yard in order to maintain the value of the home that you will own in a few short years. If your toilet gets clogged or the dishwasher stops working you don't get to phone your landlord to fix the problem. You will either have to fix the issue yourself or call a repairman, or you may even be required to replace the broken appliance. This is why the home inspection is so important when choosing your home. You don't want to choose a house that has major structural problems or is going to require a new roof in the near future as it is you, the tenant-buyer, who is responsible for these costs.

4. Small financial risk.

Buying a home is a big responsibility and entering into a rent-to-own program is no different. You need to have steady employment with a steady income and expect to live in the community for at least three years or you should just continue renting until things are more stable. If you drop out of your rent-to-own program and don't buy the house you will forfeit either part or all of the Option Credits you have paid, depending on the contract that you signed. This is similar to losing your deposit if you sign a contract to purchase a home and then back out at the last minute. If you work with an experienced rent-to-own company, are committed to the program and follow the steps laid out for you to repair your credit, the risks of having to drop out of the program are extremely small. A good rent-to-own company will take each situation on a case-by-case basis and if you do have to drop out through no fault of your own, you may get some of your Option Credit money back.

While there are some risks, or disadvantages, of a rent-to-own program, in my opinion the advantages that we talked about in Chapter 6 far outweigh the disadvantages. As long as you are aware of the disadvantages there should be no surprises.

Chapter Eight:

Rent-to-Own Process in Detail

We briefly discussed what rent-to-own is in Chapter Four. In this chapter, I we will go into more detail on each of the 15 steps of a typical rent-to-own program.

Step One. Pick a reputable and experienced rent-to-own company to work with.

If you live in a larger city in Canada or the United States, there's likely at least one rent-to-own company in your local area. If you live in a medium-sized or smaller town, there may be only one company or no local company that does rent-to-own. There is almost certainly a company in your state or province that would be willing to work with you, however. The important thing is to pick a company that has enough experience to ensure that your rent-to-own process is successful. Most rent-to-own companies will have a website, and may run ads in Craigslist, Kijiji, and the local newspaper or Facebook.

These are all great ways to find a rent-to-own company. Like anything else, do you research, find testimonials, et cetera, and if possible talk to one of the tenant buyers of the company that you're considering working with.

Step Two. Submit an application.

Most companies will have an initial application for you to fill out. This may be found online on their website, or you may have to request the application via email. This application will ask for basic information, like what your current address is, where you are considering buying, and basic questions about your current financial situation. The rent-to-own company will contact you and set up an initial interview.

Step Three. Initial interview.

Your initial interview may be face-to-face, or it may be via Skype, FaceTime, or even just a phone interview. The initial interview is to determine whether you may be a good candidate for a rent-to-own program, and to gain further information. It's also an opportunity for you to ask any questions that you may have about the rent-to-own process. You will be asked if you have any money saved up for a down payment. All rent-to-own deals will require some money put down as a deposit on your part. This is called the Initial Option Credit, or option consideration. This may be a fixed number, such as $10,000, or may be a percentage of the purchase price of your home, typically in the 3 percent to 5 percent range. You will also be asked what your gross income (income before taxes) is.

Step Four. Initial Approval.

If everything from your application and initial interview looks good and you decide to go ahead with the program, you will be given "initial approval."

Step Five. Meet with the Mortgage Broker.

After initial approval, you will meet with a mortgage broker or credit repair specialist. They will go into further detail into your financial situation, and determine if you are likely to be successful in obtaining a mortgage at the end of the program. They will also educate you on the steps required to repair or improve your credit rating. You will be asked to provide a number of documents for this meeting. These will likely include an employment letter, confirming your employment and your salary and income, two to three years of tax returns, as well as bank statements. The mortgage broker or credit specialist will pull your credit report and go over the contents of it with you in detail. If everything checks out, you will then be given "final approval."

Step Six. Final approval.

If you receive final approval, this means that the rent-to-own company believes that you have a very good chance of completing the program and becoming a homeowner in just a few short years. If for some reason you are not approved, the company will often tell you the exact steps you need to take to get final approval and they will likely invite you to reapply in the future once those steps have been taken.

Step Seven. Meet with a Realtor and find the home of your choice.

Yes, that's correct. **You get to choose the house that you want to move into,** within the price range that you have been approved for by the mortgage broker. Once you've chosen your future house, all the usual steps of buying a home will take place. An offer will be made, and the final price of the house will be negotiated. An appraisal and home inspection will be done. This is an extremely important point in the process. The home inspection will give a detailed report of the condition of the home you are considering buying and will give a list of any deficiencies or potential problems with the home. Because you, the tenant buyer, are responsible for all maintenance and repairs during the RTO process, and because you will eventually become the owner of the home, it is vitally important that you are aware of the condition of the home. It may be possible to get the seller to repair any deficiencies, or reduce the purchase price of the home to account for the costs of fixing the deficiencies. The inspection report also allows you to anticipate any repairs that are likely to be required in the near future. You will likely want to avoid any house that has any major structural/foundation problems or is likely going to require the roof or furnace system to be replaced in the near future.

Step Eight. Sign a bunch of contracts.

Your rent-to-own specialist will have a bunch of paperwork and contracts for you to fill out and sign. A good rent-to-own specialist will suggest that you have a lawyer look over all the paperwork before you sign, and I strongly suggest that you do this. I would also suggest that you find a lawyer that specializes in real estate and is familiar with the rent-to-own process. They should go over everything with you in detail, and help you understand everything that you are signing. One warning: Just because someone is a lawyer doesn't mean they understand the rent-to-own process. I've seen some lawyers advise their clients not to proceed with the rent-to-own process just because of the disadvantages that we discussed in chapter seven. They failed to see the many advantages of the program and for that reason, some people have walked away from a good RTO deal at the last moment. I suspect most of these people are still renters.

We will talk about the two main contracts here.

The first contract is just the standard Lease or Rental Agreement, much like the one you've already signed if you are currently renting. The only difference is that the term or length of the lease will match the term of the rent-to-own process that you have been approved for, usually three years.

The second contract is the Option to Buy Contract or just Option Contract. This is the contract that transforms your typical rental into a rent-to-own deal. This contract states that you have the option, but not the obligation, to buy the house for a predetermined amount (the final purchase price) on a predetermined date, usually three years later. This is important to understand.

The predetermined price means that the seller cannot raise the sale price for any reason, even if the house appreciates more than was expected. How is the final purchase price calculated? If we go back to our $300,000 example, and assume 4 percent appreciation per year, the final purchase price will be $337,460 after three years. This is calculated by multiplying $300,000 by 1.04 or 104% to get $312,000. Do this two more times to get $337,460.

The Option means that you have the choice to buy the home or not with no legal repercussions. Choosing not to buy the house is generally not a good idea because you will lose all or part of your Initial and Monthly Option Credit, but at least you cannot be sued for breaking a contract. If you were to break a regular purchase agreement, you would not only lose your deposit, but the seller can also sue you for damages, which can cost tens or hundreds of thousands of dollars. The Option Contract allows you to walk away with a relatively small penalty and no risk of legal action.

Step Nine. The investor buys the house you have chosen.

The rent-to-own company will have an investor ready and willing to buy the house you have chosen. The investor will be on title for the property. Technically, they will be your landlord for the period of the rent-to-own process, but in reality it will be your rent-to-own specialist that you will deal directly with. You may not even ever meet the investor directly.

You may ask, "What does the investor get out of the RTO process?" They get five main things:

One, positive monthly cash flow from the rent that you pay each month.

Two, mortgage pay down for the three-year term of the deal.

Three, they get the predetermined appreciation built into the deal.

Four, they get the satisfaction of knowing that they have helped a person or family realize their dream of home ownership.

Five, they get the certainty that they will get their money out of the deal in three to four years.

Step Ten. Pay a non-refundable Initial Option Credit.

The investor is going to want to see some initial investment on your part to help ensure that you are not just going to walk away from the deal, leaving the investor with a house that they don't really want. This is what investors call having "skin in the game." The initial option credit is similar to a down payment, but is usually less than what you would have to pay a bank. This could be a flat fee, such as $10,000 to $15,000, or it could be a set percentage of the purchase price, such as 3 percent to 5 percent. This initial option credit will be returned to you at the end of the program to go towards your down payment to the bank, plus any closing costs.

Step Eleven. Move into your new home!

Finally you get to move into your own home, and hopefully this will be the last move you have to make for a long, long time. You now get to set up your home the way you like it. You can make minor repairs and upgrades, but remember you are in the process of repairing your credit and saving for your down payment, so any large projects or purchases should wait until the rent-to-own term is over and you officially own the home.

Step Twelve. Pay your monthly rent as well as your Monthly Option Credit.

Your rent payment allows you to rent the house as per your lease agreement. The monthly option credit is the money you will pay on top of your rent payment that will allow you to qualify for a mortgage at the end of the RTO process. How is your Monthly Option Credit calculated? The goal of the RTO process is to accumulate 10 percent to 12 percent of the final purchase price, so you have a good down payment and can cover any closing costs, all while improving your credit rating so that you are virtually guaranteed to qualify for your own mortgage at the end of the program. The Monthly Option Credit will depend on the final purchase price and how much you put down for your Initial Option Credit, as well as the length of the term of your rent-to-own deal.

If we go back to our $300,000 example, and assume four percent appreciation per year, the final purchase price will be $337,460 after three years, as we calculated in Step Eight. Twelve percent of $337,460 is $40,495. This is the amount of money that you will need to safely qualify for a mortgage as well as cover the closing costs. If you paid $12,000 as your Initial Option Credit, the amount of money that needs to be accumulated from your Monthly Option Credits is $28,495. If we divide this number by the 36 months of the three-year program, the Monthly Option Credit would need to be $792 per month. If, however, you had a larger Initial Option Credit of $15,000 or $20,000 your Monthly Option Credit would go down considerably.

Step Thirteen. Maintain your future home.

Your future home is now your investment, maybe the largest investment you will ever make. You will want to maintain your home and yard, if you have one, to maintain or even increase the value of your investment. Most rent-to-own deals will be set up so that you, the tenant buyer, are responsible for all maintenance and repairs of the property. This is part of being a "homeowner in training." This is one reason that you must have a thorough home inspection and understand what expenses may be coming your way. All houses will have minor issues. You'll want to avoid houses that have major structural or foundation issues, or are likely to need a new roof or new HVAC (heating, ventilation, and air conditioning) in the near future, as one of these bills could jeopardize your ability to complete the rent-to-own process on time.

Step Fourteen. Follow your credit repair program.

One of the big advantages of a rent-to-own program is that you will be given the time and the specific steps to follow to build or repair your credit rating. This will involve going over your credit report in detail and fixing any issues that are negatively affecting your credit rating. Sometimes there are errors in your credit report, and you just need to notify the credit bureau to have them removed. You may find old debts that you didn't even know you have. Paying these debts can greatly improve your credit rating. Obviously you will have to make sure that you pay all of your monthly bills on time to avoid any new issues on your credit report. You can get a copy of your credit report online. The easiest way I know of is to go to www.equifax.ca. Make sure that you pay the $23.95 to get the full report, including the FICO score. This is the score that banks look at to determine whether you are a good risk for a mortgage. Your FICO score ranges from a 300 to a 900. The higher the FICO score, the more favorably the banks will look upon you. You want a score of at least 540, and preferably over 680.

To learn more about how a credit report works and how your credit report is calculated, go to www.fcac-acfc.gc.ca and search for Credit Report.

Step Fifteen. Buy your house from the investor.

This is when you finally begin reaping the benefits of home ownership that we talked about in Chapter Two. Now you could read a whole book on buying a house (and I would encourage you to do so) but I'll touch on the main points here.

With the help of a mortgage broker, hopefully the same one who has been helping you with your credit repair, you obtain a mortgage from one of the major banks or credit unions. There are some closing costs you need to be aware of. We talked about these briefly in Chapter Three. These closing costs should have been accounted for in your Initial Option Credit and Monthly Option Credit. Luckily many of the costs have been paid for by somebody else, or are not necessary to complete the RTO process.

There are no realtor fees, as these were paid for by the original seller three years ago.

You don't need a new home inspection unless you want one. You had one when you first moved in, and you have lived in the house for two to four years, so you should be aware of any issues.

The mortgage broker's fee is paid for by the bank or credit union.

Your bank will require an appraisal to make sure the house is worth what it is being sold for. This usually costs about $250, but the bank will typically return this fee if the mortgage goes ahead. Your mortgage broker or lawyer/notary should look after this for you, but make sure you ask.

What you will have to pay is the lawyer's fee or notary fee. A lawyer is more expensive, usually costing $1,000 to $1,500, and will take care of all of the legal paperwork to get your name transferred onto title. A notary public will cost less and is likely sufficient, assuming that a lawyer took care of the paperwork for the initial purchase by the investor.

Now for the bad news. Your bank may require "mortgage default insurance" on any mortgage with less than 20 percent down payment. Any mortgage with less than 20 percent down payment is considered a "high ratio mortgage" and is considered to be more risky by the bank. This insurance is for the bank's benefit (through companies such as CMHC) but unfortunately is paid by you. The closer you get to a 20 percent down payment, the less you will have to pay, so if you can afford it, you may wish to increase your initial option credit and monthly option credit to reach a 20 percent down payment, plus closing costs. Your bank will usually roll the CMHC fee into your mortgage so you may not have to pay this up front, but it will increase your mortgage amount.

Land Transfer Taxes. All provinces, except Alberta and Saskatchewan, have a land transfer tax, which ranges between 0.5 to 3 percent of the purchase price of the house. Alberta and Saskatchewan have a much smaller fees basically to cover the cost of transferring the names on Title. Some provinces have a rebate for first time home buyers. Check with your mortgage broker to see which fees apply to you and how much they will be. In British Columbia, the land transfer tax is one percent for the first $200,000 then two percent for the remainder of the purchase price.

In our $300,000 example, the final purchase price was $337,460.

One percent of $200,000 is $2,000.

Two percent of $137,460 is $2,749 for a total of $4,749.

Chapter Nine:

How to Recognize and Avoid a Rent-to-Own Scam

In all walks of life there are people who would rather make money by being dishonest rather than running an honest business. Unfortunately, rent-to-own is no exception and because rent-to-own works on the fringes of the conventional real estate market, a few bad apples feel they can take advantage of people who are desperate to own their own home. While these scams are rare, because the average person doesn't know a lot about rent-to-own, when they hear of a scam they may paint all rent-to-own with the same brush. If you just Google rent-to-own, somewhere on the first or second page there will be a story of a rent-to-own scam. This is unfortunate, as the vast majority of rent-to-own companies are honest and really have the tenant buyer's best interest at heart.

How do these scams work?

The most common one is accepting someone in a rent-to-own deal who in reality has little or no hope of qualifying for a mortgage, taking their deposit, charging a high rent, and then waiting for the tenant buyer to fail. The tenant buyer gets evicted and they lose all the money that was supposed to go toward their down payment.

How do they ensure you fail?

First, in the "small print" of the contract they will have a clause that states that if you are even one day late on a single payment then you forfeit all funds and are subject to eviction. Then they make sure you fail by selling you a house that's too expensive, or making the term of the deal to short to properly repair your credit. They also charge such a high monthly rent that if some unexpected expense comes up, you are virtually guaranteed to fall behind on your payments. Again, you get evicted and lose all your money.

In an even bolder scam, they may try to sell you a house that they don't even own.

How do you avoid these dirt bags?

This is where a little knowledge and due diligence go a long way. Having a good understanding of the rent-to-own process will allow you to sense when something is not quite right. A good rent-to-own company will ask for detailed financial information. If they are not asking for detailed financial information, how can they determine if you qualify for the program?

If the initial down payment is too small or the term of the contract is too short you should be suspicious and ask why. It takes time and money to qualify for a mortgage so it too little time or too little money is accumulated, you will never qualify for a mortgage.

They either won't answer or won't have a good answer to your questions.

These scams usually use the same house over and over again so have a realtor look into the history of the home.

Most of these scams start with a house first rent-to-own process. That is one of the reasons I strongly suggest the tenant first scenario.

Here are seven ways to avoid a rent-to-own scam.

1. Unless you know the seller very well, you should opt for the tenant first rent-to-own process. With tenant first, you will work with a whole team of professionals, the rent-to-own specialist, a realtor, mortgage broker, et cetera. A quick search of each one of these people should show that they are legitimate professionals. It would be very difficult or almost impossible to set up a scam that involved this many professionals.

2. Research the rent-to-own company. Look at their website. Honest rent-to-own companies will have a website, scammers likely will not. Google the company and all of the professionals that you work with. Look for testimonials. Some rent to own companies will have a list of current or former clients that you can contact.

3. Confirm the financial plan and credit repair program. You may want to pay a mortgage broker for a second opinion regarding the credit repair program and the likelihood that you will qualify for a mortgage at the end of the term period. They should be able to tell you whether the plan is realistic or not.

4. A good rent-to-own company will suggest you get independent legal advice. Even if they don't, GET INDEPENDENT LEGAL ADVICE. Try to find a real estate lawyer and preferably one who is familiar with rent-to-own. Just because someone is a lawyer doesn't mean they understand the rent-to-own process. I've seen people walk away from a good rent-to-own deal just because they consulted a lawyer who wasn't familiar with the rent-to-own and therefore advised them against it.

5. If you are doing a house first rent-to-own, have a Realtor check into the sales history of the house. If you can, talk to the neighbors to get a sense of what has been going on at the house. Scammers will often use the same house over and over again and the neighbors will likely have a good idea that something funny is going on.

6. Trust your instincts. It's good to be a little skeptical and trust your gut instincts. A good rent-to-own company will be happy to meet with you face to face and answer any questions you may have. If you get a bad feeling, do more research or just walk away and find another company.

7. If you're dealing directly with a seller in a house first process, have a lawyer do a "title" search to be certain the person offering you the rent-to-own actually owns the home. Also have your lawyer look over all the contracts before you sign and have any clauses changed or removed that void the contract with late payments less than two weeks.

Don't let this chapter scare you off. As I said, rent-to-own scams are extremely rare. These seven steps will ensure that the rent-to-own process you are entering into is a legitimate one and should set you up for success on your journey to becoming a homeowner.

Epilogue

So what happened to our friends Trish and Wayne from Chapter One? Spoiler alert. There is a happy ending.

With a new child on the way Trish and Wayne realized they needed a bigger place. Still stinging from being turned down for a mortgage by the bank, they began looking on Craigslist for a new place to rent when they came across an advertisement for a Rent-to-Own company in their area. After looking up and learning about rent-to-own and researching the company they contacted the company, filled out an application and set up an initial consultation.

With the $15,000 they had in savings and only moderately bruised credit, they were approved for a three year program with a maximum price of $340,000. A credit repair program was set up that should have their credit rating above 680 by the end of the three year program

They called their Realtor and it turns out the house that they wanted so badly was still on the market! The rent-to-own company went to work and got an accepted offer for $295,000. Five thousand dollars less than their original offer! The company had an investor *already lined up and pre-approved for a mortgage of that size. The inspection revealed a few small issues with the house that the seller agreed to fix before the closing date.*

Trish and Wayne moved in and they went to work painting the third bedroom and getting it ready for their new baby scheduled to arrive only two months later.

Now, two years later, they are well on their way to owning their own home. Their credit ratings have steadily improved and between their Initial Option Credit of $15,000 and the Monthly Option Credit they have been paying each month, they will have a down payment of ten percent and will easily cover their closing costs.

Now, if you made it all the way to the end of this book, I assume you are at least curious whether rent-to-own could work for you or someone you know. If you are ready to get out of the rental cycle, here is your call to action:

1. Go to Equifax.ca and download a copy of your credit report and get your FICO score.

2. Contact a local Mortgage Broker and find out if you qualify now to get your own mortgage.

3. If not, search for a Rent-to-Own company in your area and set up your no pressure and no obligation initial consultation to find out if rent-to-own could work for you and your family.

If you are in British Columbia or Alberta and would like to work with our company, look us up at:

www.BCRTO.com

Facebook at BC Rent to Own Homes.

Otherwise, you can contact us and we may be able to help you find a good rent-to-own company near you.

About the Author

David Fenton is a Canadian board certified radiologist and Associate Professor of Radiology at the University of British Columbia. He has worked as a radiologist for over a decade at St. Paul's Hospital in Vancouver, BC.

An active real estate investor, David is the founder of BC Rent to Own Homes which helps families who don't qualify for bank financing realize their dream of home ownership in as little as two years.

One hundred percent of the proceeds of this book and a portion of the profits from his company are donated to Habit for Humanity to help rebuild in Nepal after devastating earthquakes in April and May 2015.

www.ingramcontent.com/pod-product-compliance
Lightning Source LLC
Chambersburg PA
CBHW070050210526
45170CB00012B/643